Calendar of Dust

BENJAMIN ALIRE SÁENZ

Calendar of Dust

Broken Moon Press · Seattle

Some of these poems appeared (in slightly different forms) in
*Puerto del Sol, The Seattle Review, Tonantzín,
Sequoia, Poetry East,* and *Saguaro.*

Printed in the United States of America.

ISBN 0-913089-16-8
Library of Congress Catalog Card Number: 90-86380

Cover photograph and internal images, *Puye Cliff Dwellers,*
copyright © 1990 by Patricia Ridenour.
Used by permission of the artist.

Broken Moon Press
Post Office Box 24585
Seattle, Washington 98124-0585 USA

I bequeath myself to the dirt
to grow from the grass I love . . .
WALT WHITMAN

In memory of my niece,
Amy Aileen Houser
September 23, 1976–February 10, 1990

Contents

III

Resurrections

Acknowledgements

I would like to thank the Creative Writing Department at Stanford University for awarding me a two-year fellowship which enabled me to complete this work. I would like to express my gratitude to Nancy Packer, Gay Pierce, Kathy Ganas, and Gail Perez. I am particularly indebted to Ken Fields, Jose Antonio Burciaga, and Arturo Islas: good writers, all of them—and the very best of teachers. I owe a special thanks to W.S. DiPiero, who gave me his support and his thoughtful and engaged criticism.

Anne Neelon and Rosemary Catacalos are poets gifted with good minds and even better hearts—I kept their voices close to me as I wrote many of these poems. I owe a special debt of gratitude to Larry Schmidt, the calmest man I have ever known—and one of the most gifted. My work is all the better for what he gave.

Most especially I would like to thank Denise Levertov. Despite her many commitments, she always took the time to read my poems with care. She had faith in my vision, challenged me to make my poems true, and set an example of excellence. The debt I owe her can never be repaid.

Lastly, I would like to thank the members of my family. They have been my truest teachers. They are the people who taught me to endure losses, express rage, and embrace the life that has been given me. In a word, they gave me God.

I
————

Exiles

Creation

====

Trinity Site, New Mexico
5:30 A.M., July 16, 1945

"Let there be light."
And there was light.

The sun was slow in arriving that morning
though it was no longer dark, was light enough,
and having been born with good eyes, we could see.
We stood on the cool cactus sand which was once
an ocean with a patience we rarely practiced.
It was hard to imagine so much water in this place
of permanent thirst. Motionless, we stood
just as we once waited for our sons to struggle
out of our wives. The labor wasn't long,
but the longest ten seconds of our lives. Ten
seconds, that was all—
        And then the man-made flash—
twice as large as the sun—photographed the moment
in fire. Flames burning the sands,
slashing the face of the calm.
        The ball of thunder strangled
the sky. Reached, blasted, bounced on rocks,
became a perfect tower—taller, wider, whiter
than the Aztecs ever dreamed of or desired.
All the gilded temples where we crossed ourselves
and worshipped perished in the smoke. Everything
surpassed in the new incense. Falling.
On our knees. It seemed to reach for us.
We prayed for it to stop, yet urged it on.

The air exploded hot, grew cold, then hot again
invoking Indian winds to rise, to blow,
to break the earth in half.
     Then it was silent.
Motionless, we stood—the air throwing us
back, and we remembered our selves, our past,
the boyhood houses filled with women's singing.
We rose, surveyed the aftermath of our great
experiment. There was not much damage:
rearranged sand, uprooted bushes, a few dead
rabbits. This was, after all, already a desert,
already named *Jornada del Muerto*, plain
of the no-personed God.
     We had seen. And lived.
We blessed ourselves, smelling the victory.
We put on jubilant smiles in the face
of the outcome. But the smiles fell off
unable to withstand the great success.

     The sun was slow in arriving that morning.
Those of us who bore witness saw it rise
in the new sky, motionless, but it no longer
gave enough light. Now, after many years,
our eyes have grown accustomed to the dark.

Exiled

Matagorda, Texas
Summer, 1856

I

"They're calling
a big meeting. Teresa heard them
when she served their lunch."

"Meeting? So?"

"A *big* meeting."

"How big is big?"

"Big enough to be bad."

"For who?"

"For us."

"Ahh, Teresa's *patron* likes to talk.
Rich boss, reads books, likes to think
he's God. Sometimes, they get bored,
get together, make noise
like aging chickens.
They like meetings, words, and laws,
the gringo. I know how
they think—comes to nothing."

"This time they're going to
make laws—about us. Make
us illegal. Out—
we'll be out. Or dead."

"Who's gonna plant their seeds,
plow their fields?
Who's gonna feed their cows,
cook their food?"

"Money. Money can buy.
It can hire,
can fire, can do
somersaults,
can name the trees
and stars. Money
is a wind, and we
are candles.
It wants our flames
blown out."

"We don't live
in the same part of town,
we work their lands,
come home,
don't bother them.
We even bow our heads
when they pass,
make them think
they're smarter,
better lookin'."

"But when they see us
they think we move
like *coyotes*, and dread
the day we'll do more
than howl.
They'll never like us."

"Likc? Who givcs
a stinkin' carcass
whether they like us
or not. We don't
like them either.
You think they're afraid
of us? They own.
Plantations and gardens—
and bedrooms
as big as our homes.
They have us
where they want.
A meeting will change
nothing."

"You think you know
how they think? You don't.
They hate.
Teresa and I are packing."

"You gonna run
like a scared deer?"

"The deer—God
gave him good legs. Grace.
Teresa and I want to live.
We'll use our legs and move."

"They'll have to kill me.
I'll leave my blood
on their white shirts,
leave my smell
in their hearts.

I'll be dead
before I'll be illegal.
And they'll remember
my name. My legs
were not born for running.
I'll stay. I'll stay."

"The buffalo, he stayed.
He's gone."

"The buffalo was stupid,
small brain. Me, I
think—a man.
Stay. We'll fight.
Stay. The day has come."

"They own the land."

"The land was ours—
and then they came."

"And before
was someone else's.
Ask the Indian,
he will tell you
the land belongs to no one.
Use your legs to run."

II

MATAGORDA—The people of Matagorda County have held a meeting and ordered every Mexican to leave the county. To strangers this may seem wrong, but we hold it to be perfectly right and highly necessary; but a word of explanation should be given. In the first place, then, there are none but the lower class or "peon" Mexicans in the county; secondly, they have no fixed domicile, but hang around the plantations, taking the likeliest negro girls for wives; and thirdly, they often steal horses, and these girls, too, and endeavor to run them to Mexico. We should rather have anticipated an appeal to Lynch law, than the mild course which has been adopted.

III

Ramón and Teresa
traveled on the side
of the dirt road,
no hurry
in their young feet.
Having walked miles,
she stopped, sat
on the road and wept.
He sat next to her
combing her black
hair with his fingers:

"Tears?
Teresa no llores.
Do not waste good water—
we will need it for the long walk."
He wiped her face
with his palms.

"And where will
we walk? *México?*"

"Who is left there?
Our parents were buried
on this side of the river."

"But they do not
want us in Texas."

"It does not matter
what they want.
We are *Tejanos*,
Teresita. *Tejanos*."

"They will give us
no place, Ramón."

He broke
into laughter:
"They cannot rob us
of our feet."

She laughed with him, rose
taking his hand
as brown as the Texas ground.
They continued
walking north,
walked in silence,
the desert before them.

Walking

El Paso, Texas
1976

I am walking down the street:

I see a woman and whisper,
"Yes, there she is,
I have found her. She
is the one who can tell me
where I live."
I speak to her. She smiles
and we have dinner. She gives
me her phone number. We part.
I walk out—into the street
and feel the night
pushing its tongue
down my throat.
I try to breathe,
and find a phone booth
to call her, but
throw the number away
when my fingers touch
the dial. She does not
know where I live.

Happily, may I walk,
Happily, with abundant showers, may I walk.
Happily, with abundant plants, may I walk.

I see a man with a book,
his eyes leaping out
like scattering frogs.
He tells me my name
is written in the book.
I ask him if the book
contains my address.
He shakes his head:
"Hell!" he yells, "your
address is in hell!"
I say, "No."
I walk away.
"Heaven!" he shouts,
"your address is in heaven!"
No. He does not
know where I live.

Happily, on the trail of pollen, may I walk.
Happily, may I walk.

An old woman, wrinkled
and wadded up like the torn
pages of a discarded book
carries a bag and tells me
I have a nice suit.
She nods. She claws
the cloth and rubs
my coat, a magic lamp.
I reach into my pockets
and give her money.
She tastes it. I ask
her where she lives.

"Where I live?" Her words
fall to the sidewalk
like the last leaves of life.
She walks away. She does not
know where I live.

May it be beautiful behind me.
May it be beautiful below me.
May it be beautiful above me.

I am thinking of me
when I was a boy. The boy
once lived in a house
and he used to sing day songs.
There was only one road
in the town where he lived
so he never got lost
and running was easy,
and all the watermelons
in the world were his.
But the pink taste,
the farmer's sugar
in his hungry mouth,
and the seeds he swallowed
did not grow inside him.
And now
even walking is hard
because the city is not
streetless   but songless.

Journeys

El Paso/Juárez
1984

Every day she crosses. She
has been here before, has passed these streets
so often she no longer notices the shops
nor their names nor the people. No longer
notices the officials at the bridge who let her
pass as if she were going shopping. They know
her, know where she's going, do not ask questions.
They have stopped smiling at each other.
Each morning she walks from her
Juárez home, crosses the bridge to El Paso.
Downtown, she waits for a bus that takes her
to a house where she irons and cleans and cooks.
She is not afraid to get caught. The Border
Patrol does not stop her as she waits for
the bus after work. They know what she does,
know she has no permit—but how would it look
arresting decent people's maids? How
would it look? And besides, she's a woman
getting old. The *Migra* prefers to chase
young men. She no longer notices their green
vans. They do not exist for her.
Nor she, for them.
        She does not mind the daily journeys,
not far, and "really," she says to herself,
"it is all one city, Juárez and El Paso.

The river is small and tired. A border? Ha!"
She sits, she laughs, she catches her bus to go home.
    The woman whose house she cleans
asked her once if she wanted to be an American.
"No," she smiled, "I'm happy." What for,
she thought, what for? My children, they want
to live here. Not me. I belong in my Juárez.
    She cooks, she cleans, she takes her bus.
She journeys every day. The journey is easy,
never takes a long time, and always it is sunny.
When it rains, the people who live here
praise God—but she, she curses him
for the spit that soaks her skin.

Parades

Navajo Native Lands, New Mexico–Arizona
Summer, 1863–Winter, 1864

I can take no pride in this fearful destruction. My sleep
is haunted by dreams of starving Navajo squaws and children.
If the elders of the tribe would listen to reason, we could
make peace. But they're stubborn men, so I must finish
what I have started.
                                        KIT CARSON

I

Taos in June.
Leaving Taos
in June.
Leaving Taos
in a parade of song.
The line, straight, tall,
Colonel Carson leading
officers, men, wagons.
Mules, howitzers, horses.
A song in June:

Come dress your ranks, my gallant souls,
A-standing in a row,
Kit Carson he is waiting
To march against the foe;
At night we march to Moqui
O'er hills of snow,

To meet and crush the savage foe:
Bold Johnny Navajo.
Johnny Navajo!
O Johnny Navajo!

II

"Surrender and you will be led
to new lands where you will live
in peace." White pages asked for an answer.
No answer came. None surrendered.

New Man was smart, systematic, spared nothing.
Camping on Navajo lands, Carson moved his troops:
the trees that bore fruit, they cut;
they dug up plants that gave berries
or nuts—emptied the earth of roots—
there would be no resurrections. Burned
every summer pasture,
burned every field of grass,
burned every corn and wheatfield.
No blade of green escaped.
The land was clothed in ashes.

III

The Navajo fled in silence,
reached their cliffs, their sacred place:
Canyon de Chelly.

Little to eat but piñon nuts,
berries of yucca, wild potatoes.
But there, an orchard of peach trees.
The Navajo lived.

The Navajo read the stars,
saw the apocalypse,
pled for reason.
The New Man said:
"Leave your land or starve."
Navajo voices answered:
"This is not reason!"
None surrendered.

IV

Winter's frozen earth gave little food.
They lived in silence and hiding.
Unable to walk in the land of the living,
they entered the dwellings of the dead.
Penitents, they entered the grave grounds
asking forgiveness for the great disturbance.
They lived in silence and prayer,
their voices fading to whispers.
By night, they ventured from hiding
to harvest frozen peaches
from their last garden.

Into the land of the sacred,
Carson followed, white cloud
of destruction. No mercy
for stubborn Indians.

The valley filled with voices,
the strange tongue
of the New Man.

New Man cut down the last orchard.
Three hundred trees, chopped down,
set ablaze, warming winter skies.
From hidden sanctuaries,
the Navajo
smelled incense
of burning peaches.

V

They arrived on foot.
Eight thousand starving souls
arrived at the gates
of New Man's fortress.
No tears on either side.

A winter's march.
Leaving their lands,
the songless walk of the
conquered. A tattered line:
warriors, women,
sons and daughters marching.

Three hundred and fifty miles
on foot. They marched
through a desert, named it
"land of no shadows."

Soldiers surrounding them,
straight, tall,
on horseback.
When women died,
too sick
to take a further step,
the New Man cut off their breasts
and tossed them in the air.

Poem

Las Cruces, New Mexico
July 9, 1985

This is my Letter to the World
That never wrote to Me . . .

Life wrote no poems
for you.
You thought we
locked your name
in closets,
hiding your face
in the back of our albums.
We were all so normal,
the six later arrivals,
rivals to the first born,
the oldest male:
gay and Chicano,
nothing worse than that.
We, the normal
sons and daughters
with talked-about lives,
never went inside your clubhouses.
Instead, we marched straight
into the New Mexico sky
like little rows of cotton
one after another
flying out of the same warm womb
and raised our hands,
sometimes praying, sometimes clenched,
towards the Catholic God we worshipped.

Life wrote no poems
for you.
No pretty words to help
you sleep.
No lullabies for the diseased.
The morning dew
on the ground settled late,
left early
let nothing grow.
You lie in that garden.

Unseen people
sent flowers when you died.
We were listed as
your survivors
in a yellowing page
of a newspaper
that we no longer read.
We outlived your secrets,
outlived your public dreams:
we placed those childhood toys
inside your casket.
We, six surviving siblings
with strange tears,
went to your funeral
and asked,
"Died of what
at thirty-eight?"

Brothers and sisters,
but nothing in common
with you
except a mother's wounded womb
and her scarred voice
whispering novenas
to the brown-faced God—
a woman's prayers
pushing us up
towards a ragged sainthood.
We will inherit her house.
You, the oldest male,
have inherited what?

Donaciano, your still
distant name
is a seed
lost in grains of sand. Buried
no water there
to make you green
to give you roots
to pull you towards the sky.

The Dead

Southwestern New Mexico
10,000 B.C. — 1150 A.D.

I

From Asia, you crossed a bridge of land,
now called the Bering Strait, now swallowed
in water. No human steps to follow,
you slowly found your way on pathless grounds—
untouched, unseen, untrampled. Your lungs, growing
like grass, lived and breathed an air as soft as clouds.
Swimming, drinking, bathing. You, in wombs of water
blue as morning skies. The rain was clean then.
Travelers lost in time—walking, chanting,
dancing—tracks on mapless earth, no man-made lines,
no borders. Arriving not in ships, with no supplies,
waving no flags, claiming nothing, naming
no piece of dirt for wealthy lords of earth.

You did not come to own; you came to live.

Hunting huge mammoths, you killed to eat,
survive. In time, the mammoth died.
You lived, continued moving—southward.
Days and days of walking, the earth memorizing
your steps—walking, sometimes stopping,
perhaps pausing to pray, to dream, to wonder.
Your eyes *saw:* buffalo, deer, birds—
your hands leaving portraits on rocks.
Explorers, nomads never settling—
ephemeral camps your home until your legs gave out.

You sat and breathed the air, the arid dust,
planting your feet in the desert.
It rained—and there your roots grew deep.

Ten thousand years. Ten thousand years before resting.

II

From yellow hills, you viewed the growing trees.
Wet grounds, smells of green, you reached for it.
You drank from river's water, knew what to eat,
knew which seeds to plant. You plowed rows
with hands; dug ditches with hands. Things grew.
Gardens. Rows weaving the ground into rugs—patterns
of Spring. The lines in leaves of corn, deep
as the lines of your palms. You learned to build:
clay and water, and sun to bake the bricks
like fire baked your bread. You built from mud,
earth above you, earth below you. By earth
surrounded. And there, your children played, there
your children grew. There, your children learned.

Like corn, your towns grew tall. Fruitful, you multiplied.

Soon, you were many. Villages speaking your language.
Occupied hands, laborers on the land—hearts
aching for more. Listening to rains, and winds, and wolves—
you told stories. Stories of wandering fathers—spoken—
you left no books. But pots. Molded clay, you formed
perfect bowls. Pots to cook, to carry crops, plates
to hold your food. Your hearts ached for more. And then
your artist's eyes taught working hands to paint.

You found plants that bled color; formed brushes, imagined
worlds—stories—beavers, bears, bugs; men and fish together;
quail, corn, deer; hands holding flowers; lightning, birds—
and then the drought. No rain. No rain for years.

The river dried. You perished in the dust.

III

Mimbreños.
You buried your ancestors
in floors beneath your homes.
You slept on them,
you kept them with you always.
They grew through earthen floors
filling your lives
with dreams of passing worlds.

Mimbreños.
You buried ancestors
placed your art in their graves—
heads carefully covered in clay bowls.
Each painted work, pure, calm,
luminous
                        and in a moment of prayer
                        or rage
you broke a hole
piercing your work. A hole

to free the tired spirits
of those who gave you breath
and to remind your grieving eyes
that without them,
nothing, not even your bowls,
could be perfect.

Mimbreños.
Builders, farmers, potters.
People of the *Mimbres,*
the trees that grew there
where you lived.
The willows, young,
bent in the wind,
but grew too fast, too strong.
The drought wind broke their limbs.

Mimbreños.
The world, like your burial bowls, has a hole.
It is a space, a wound, a song
that says your feet, your hands
no longer walk, nor plant, nor paint
upon this breaking earth.

Aftermath

San Francisco
October 17, 1989

At night, there are rumblings,
faint, then loud. The sound then
recedes like a wave—mumblings
of an earth settling down again

like first-time lovers tangled
in twisted sheets, caught
working to free themselves.
After the seconds-long climax,

quick and angry as it was,
they have fallen in each other's
paths, disturb each other's
rest, bump and bruise

smother each other's dreams.
Cursing the darkness, lost in
the aftermath, both of them asking
why they were caught unprepared

for this endless night, not even
a candle to give them light.
Their nervous breathing almost
words: *this is not love, this*

act we have committed. How
could we have allowed our bodies
to rage against each other?
That anger, hidden for years, had

been kept locked until it was
let loose in their sex—and yet
they had always known it was
knocking, waiting to be torn open.

.

The quieting earth is turning
uncomfortable in its new position.
Tired insomniac uttering moans
of sorrow and repentance, begging

to return to the old dispensation—
but that which has been loosed
cannot be bound again, and must
remain unloosed. Once the apple

is bitten, it has been bitten.
We know this story, have memorized
the ending by heart: once stripped
we are exposed, ashamed, and we are

condemned to carry what is left
of ourselves into exile, no longer
allowed to step on stable grounds.
An easy sleep, after this, will

not come. Sleep, after this, will
resemble the labor of the day.
Night will no longer be still,
will groan, will grunt, will sway.

II

Lamentations

The Book of Lamentations

The Mexican is living proof that the Indians
mated with the buffalo.
A bathroom wall in Palo Alto

I

My mother taught me a poem
in that time of life when I was losing
my first set of teeth:
Sol, sol, toma este diente
dame otro mejor . . .
It was a plea
to the god of drought
to send a new, strong tooth.
I sang the psalm
and tossed the tooth
towards cloudless skies
expecting my voice to be heard.

II

In a library, I read thick books,
dusty, smelling of always blowing winds.
John Winthrop believed the English
had more claim to the land than the Natives.
Mary Rowlandson's captivity
was a barbarous public act exposing true
colors of treacherous Indian hearts.
She held fast to her faith, and wrote
the first American best-seller upon her

prayed-for release. God was English.
Hernán Cortés disagreed. God was Spanish.
The Indians did not enter the debate.

III

Headlines in the news this summer:
     Sixteen men locked in a railroad car
while being smuggled by a *coyote*.
Sixteen men suffocated
swallowing each other's air,
the *coyote* dying with them
in communion.
     Women, names and eyes erased,
were being shoveled up—
mouths filled with silence and sand.
     Two brothers drowning.
The watchers gathered, pointing at the place.
And the river smiling for the camera.

IV

Again, in the room of the quiet library,
I read more books, the dust from their words
like flies around a carcass.
In 1537, a Papal Bull proclaimed the Indians human.
A century later, the imprimatured humans,
exiled from lands once theirs,
found a place and claimed it for themselves.
Ysleta. The village grew. Ysleta.
Its streets hardened by droughts, by winds—

34

hammers pounding the dirt; its blood mingling.
Spanish, Native, Mexican, Mestizo.
New wars, new laws, new borders
claimed it county seat. In 1883, Easterners arrived,
looked around, found other sites for homes.
They moved the county seat,
kept it in El Paso's newer buildings.
Ysleta: brown streets empty as the river
in the winter. El Paso:
streets busy, clean and white.

V

Last month, in the finest day of Spring,
I went to the bathroom in a public library.

The graffiti on the wall said Mexicans
were the color of solid human shit.

VI

My mother taught me a rhyme
in that time of life when I was losing
my first set of teeth:
"*Sol, sol*," I sang, "*Sol, sol . . .*"
I thought the sun could catch.
I thought the sun had hands.

A New Flag

Las Vegas, New Mexico
August 15, 1846

I have more troops than I need to overcome any opposition
which you may be able to make against us . . .

GENERAL KEARNY

Unbending in the sun, he faced
East, then West. Faced North, then
South. All directions met his eyes
in stillness. He climbed atop
the highest roof, and with a breath

erased the former borders. The old
dispensation, banished. Mexico's
claims as false as the claims of
the Navajo. *We come as protectors,*
friends to the quiet and peaceful.

The brown eyes of the town
were gathered to pay homage
to the new Cortés. The masses
in the plaza lifted their eyes
to see the eagle and serpent fall

like a tired sun. The new flag
rose great in the sky, blue as
the eyes of the general, red as
the skin of the Indian, white as
the bones of the dead. The new

priest gave his blessing:
absolved them of their mortal
sin, their allegiance to Mexico
forgiven. The anointed general
stood, the troops and cannons

behind him. *We will disturb
nothing, not a pepper, not an
onion.* A woman knelt before him.
The general, moved by her faith,
her humble gesture. She hid her

clenched fists, and cursed him
under her breath: *Not a pepper,
not an onion.* She raised her
eyes toward the god: *It is not
for the crops that I kneel.*

Teresa

Old Picacho, New Mexico
April, 1963

She was dying that windy spring
that woman with braids as thick
as her arms, that old woman whose knees
were wasted with kneeling
before statues who had memorized
the sounds of her whispers. She
was dying that windy spring.

She outlived a husband, remarried.
The second was a drunk who knew
how to make adobes, fashion
them like pots from the earth, who knew
the secret to giving her sons
and daughters, who knew nothing
of love in old age, knew nothing
of women.

She was dying that windy spring,
that woman who made shirts, made
pants, made dresses and quilts,
that old woman who canned jalapeños
in vinegar and spices, made tortillas
on an old stove burning with smells
of *mesquite* the year round
like an eternal flame—of work.
A maker like her God. A midwife,
she delivered her daughters' children.

Her hands, twisted like the roots of her herbs,
felt as soft as the cotton she picked as a girl.
She smelled of old prayer books, smelled
of old churches—wax candles
that burned into night.
Her room knew no darkness.
For twelve years, leukemia courted her
as she dreamed
while her husband moved to another bed.
Her back never bent in her sickness.
Her rooms knew no darkness.

In her seventies that spring,
that windy spring
she was dying,
that woman who was mother to my mother.

And my mother,
my mother howled to the empty
New Mexico skies:
"*No te lleves a mi mama,
no te la lleves . . .*"

That windy spring, that evening
the sun was as red as the autumn chile
she dried on her roof.

Workers

Texas

1912

We have to have a class of people
who will do this kind of labor.

In the valley
of the Rio Grande,
green with running waters,
I signed a contract
to pick cotton
with ready hands.
The planter paid
for our passage
from the city
far away.
Arriving at camp,
we were led to a chicken coop,
our new house for the season.
"No," I said, "something better,
or we will go."
"Go," the planter said.

As we prepared to leave,
the sheriff arrived
from nowhere, from the sky,
sudden as Guadalupe
appeared to Diego—
the gringo could work
such miracles.

In jail, the planter
said he'd set me free
when I paid the cost
of the passage. He
charged me twice for his trouble.
I refused, at first,
but knowing
my wife would be made to work
I paid. We left
Texas for good—
never set foot there
again. But I left
singing: *Never go back.*
Never let that Texas sky
bend my back again.
Never go back.

The Picking Season

Eloy, Arizona
August, 1988

Mama, your voice worked hard
to keep me from falling
asleep at the wheel. I drove
west through the night, tired,
but your voice, strong as coffee.
As we passed that Arizona town, you
grew quiet and whispered something
about the stars: "You can
see them all—I remember."
I kept my eyes on the wheel,
did not look up, afraid to lose
the road. We did not stop,
continued traveling into night.
"Your father and I were married
there. We came to pick cotton,
both of us following the picking
season, but the picking wasn't good
that year. It rained for days.
We made no money." You said
nothing else, your voice
escaping.

I imagine it rained
the day you both arrived
at the small courthouse.

You drove there in a beat-up car
with an engine my father re-built.
You ran from the car, hand in hand,
both of you soaked and laughing.
As you waited, you sat drying
yourselves on a bench in the dark
hallway. You sat, not speaking, no
family members to fill up the quiet
with their loud Spanish—all
of them far away. No one to stand
and witness the event, no one
to take pictures of you and my
father (who had not yet grown
his mustache). When you entered
the empty room, there were no
well-dressed friends lining the pews,
no voices singing the *Ave Maria*,
no priest to give his blessing.
I imagine my father in his cleanest
shirt (no tie)—and you wearing
a cotton dress with printed flowers.
(You would not have worn white,
would not have lied that way. You
had already known a man who'd left
you with a child.) There must
have been no ring (you've never
worn one). Maybe my father just
took your already-rough hands in his,
and held them tight as some aging
gringo pronounced you man and wife.

And afterwards you rented
a room, wondering where
to go, how to celebrate, not knowing
anyone—except each other.
And maybe that night the rain
stopped. Maybe that night
the clouds were swept away
and the sky showed you all its stars.
You said you could see them all.

The Willow

Las Cruces, New Mexico
Spring, 1964

I loved a tree in my boyhood, a tree
in my grandfather's garden, a weeping
willow whose ancient limbs longed
upwards, then arched downwards, perfect

bows which reached so low, so low
the leaves brushed the grass as if to
sweep it clean. I played alone among
the arches of leaves, pulling the green

limbs around myself as if they were the
great arms of God. They held me tight.
I was so loved in that embrace of leaves.

And then sickness came

to the garden one spring, the old willow
wrapped in a shroud of bugs. I could only
watch, could not touch it. I shouted
at the tree, and told it to live, and

though it fought to breathe without
leaves, neither my voice nor the rain
could heal it. So the tree was chopped,
stripped limb by limb until there was

only a stump. And the stump, too,
was pulled from the ground—pulled
so harshly that even the roots came up

shaking the whole garden.

Josefina

Las Cruces, New Mexico
June, 1969

I

Josefina grew peaches and mint. Josefina grew
flowers that swayed to the strong breezes of her footsteps.
In her yard, one spring, when I was four,
I cut every rose—tore them from their stems.
She chased me down the street so close
to catching me, her spit hitting the back
of my neck as she ran—yelling, neighbors
at their doors watching, she not caring.
Josefina had strong legs, knew how to run
and cuss. When her roses sprouted new blossoms
she gathered them, arranged them perfect
in a glass. Delivered them to my door.

II

Josefina spoke to statues on tired afternoons.
Josefina played games with her favorite:
Joseph, her patron saint. He held the baby Jesus
in his arms. When my uncle disappeared, she took
away his child—Joseph filling with tears in grief.
She looked at him sternly, told him his kidnapped
son would return when he earned his keep,
brought back her son. When my uncle reappeared,
came back from the drinking dead, Josefina,
good as her word, returned the missing child
to Joseph's outstretched arms—laughing. Josefina
got her way. Josefina, so much laughter.

47

III

Josefina spoke no English (though I knew she understood).
Once, a man came to her door demanding money for a debt.
"Mañana," she said, *"mañana, por favor . . ."*
"Mañana!" he yelled, "you people! Always mañana!"
She glared at him and nodded—and used the only English
I ever heard her speak: "Tomorrow. Tomorrow
is a word the gringo made *for us*. Tomorrow
is word for the poor." She shut the door,
stormed towards the kitchen to cook—pots and pans
clanging in a symphony of anger.

IV

Josefina was a seer. Before she left home
to enter the hospital for simple surgery,
she spoke of a dream—a dream where her friend,
a woman named Teresa (my other grandmother, already
dead) came to pay a visit. Teresa sat at the edge
of her bed. Teresa, *"mujer tan bonita,"* woman,
so beautiful. Teresa smiled: *"No tengas miedo."*
Woman, do not be afraid. She said Teresa
brought a message. She entered the hospital
for simple surgery. Josefina never came home.

Your Daughter

California
Winter, 1989

for Linda, my older sister

Your daughter will be bleeding soon.
You speak of this on the phone
sadly. *Just a baby,*
you say, *my little girl.*
Your voice grows still
and for a second
you travel
to that summer day in August
when you wanted to die
with joy
as you held the miracle
of your flesh.
Just a baby, you say.
The quiet in your voice
reminds me that you, too,
were once mama's
little girl.
I still remember
when you entered that country
where a younger brother
could not follow.

Your daughter will be bleeding soon.
Oh, it's come too fast, you say,
*and whatever she feels
she will keep to herself*

(her mother's daughter).
Already, hair is growing
on her arms,
her legs,
and soon she will have
hips large enough—large—larger
than any man's love.
Breasts will grow,
breasts which will someday
bloom, give milk—
woman's bud
blossoming the earth.
Her dreams will be
of boys—boys
who will dream of her, too. Boys
who will want
to swallow her.

Your daughter will be bleeding soon.
She will smell like the rain
in a drought.
Your voice
cracks in grief
for your aging self
aware that as your dark daughter
grows,
you will start to wither—
aware that you
will no longer be
the only woman
in your house.

And yet, your grief
is more than for
the passing of your time.
Your grief is for
your child
who must learn
too soon
the price she must pay
for her power.

At Thirteen

Las Cruces, New Mexico
August, 1967

At thirteen, I knew what it was to sin,
Knew what it was to love, to love the sin:
My curious hand reached down to touch
What was mine alone, rubbing

Clenching, grabbing, mesmerized
By a growing greed, something of men
Already in me, hard, harder, up and down,
Until my boyhood frenzy left me bathed

In sweat. The wet of discovery flooding
My stomach and chest, a milky rain
Of warmth from clouds within. That smell:
Moist morning cotton rose to my head.

I had to taste—so bitter awful, salty
As blood. I stretched across the bed, tired
Unable to return to my former sleep.
For a week, I could not face my father

Nor my mother, afraid that their eyes
Knew and accused. And Saturday, I ran
To church vomiting *O my God, I am heartily
Sorry for having offended thee, and I detest*

All my sins . . . My secret spilled
To forgiving priest, my voice trembling
Repentance in every word. I could have
Hid forever in dark shame. And after

Healing words, newness and light. Innocent
Once more. I knelt and prayed. Clean
And free, I went home, waited a week, then
Did it again and again—in awe of the miracle.

Ring of Life

Palo Alto, California
February, 1989

In one year, many deaths. Spring
Is born in blooms of impermanent buds,
Flowers so fragile they willingly
Fade, flowers so generous they give way

To the growing fruits of Summer—
Summer which colors the growing crops
Deeper and golden and red with such
Soft touches of sun—golden and deeper

Until they can stand it no longer
And clamor for picking, for death.
In Fall, gardens and trees that have
Survived the sledgehammer storms

Of hail, winds, floods, let go
Their cared-for children. The sweet
Crops are gathered, admired, tasted—
Tasted, and yes, painted in stillness:

Human attempts to stop the unstoppable
Cycle. In Winter, there are only frozen
Fields and branches. And though life
Is there, it hides its face like an exiled

Priest who must turn away from the world
To the monastery of sad solitude to sleep,
To rest, to pray until he has gathered
Strength enough to return to the ring

Of life—to fight again--to give again—
To love—and die again.

III

Resurrections

Crucifix

Palo Alto, California
Summer, 1988

It shone like a still sea in the stove-burner sunlight
of the Western drought. (A long drought that year
and I in the middle of it. Water everywhere in my dreams.)

It shone, a luminous stone, smooth, hard
but—to my eyes—silky, soft as skin, tender leaves
on spring trees, touched by rain. Light green pigments

mixing with pinks of early summer roses—growing
against the dull dawns, the dusty straw-yellow skies.
A garden—a sea—to be lost in. Mirage—was just

a piece of dirt, soft clay baked into hardness
created from the dust. Just an object, man-made.
It should have been enough to touch the smooth

curves which rolled like valleys and hills on its
earthen surface. It should have been enough—why
possess the clay? I took it home, placed it on a

nail in the wall. It hung like a crucifix, secure,
and though the drought continued (day and night, unbroken
chain of heat, endless calendar of dust) my thirst

subsided. When I moved, I packed my ceramic
with care, with rare patience, convinced it was protected
from all harm. When my belongings arrived in my new

home, I opened the well-taped box with my name
written on all its sides and found my ceramic in
pieces. Broken in transit. Baked earth cracks

and is lost. I picked the sharp-edged pieces from the box
like a farmer examining a harvest, surveying the season
of loss. Unable to accept the brokenness which had arrived

at my door, I began to place each fragment on the floor
until I had formed from memory the piece I purchased.
I began to glue it slowly. Hour after hour, I worked,

moved to save. I knelt on the floor—lost
in the labor like a novice begging for faith, the water
of his hurt gone dry: "Come back, come back . . ."

Alone, I lived in the silence of re-creation
until I brought it back to life. It hangs now
an awkward, crooked ceramic, a wide-cracked

sculpture that screams of an original smoothness. In its
shattered state, it is something beyond the work of its maker.
I stare at it daily, memorize the cracks, reminders of drought

and water. It hangs in my house, a crucifix of brokenness,
of fragile resurrection. It hangs—tenuously—never again
secure. Any day, it will fall from its place or again be

shattered in the movements of life. I will kneel, re-glue it,
transform it once again. It will hang forever on my wall.

Cemetery

Mesilla, New Mexico
Day of the Dead, 1988

    I walk these grassless grounds
Cracked, withering in weeds. My eyes move
From one monument to the next: a star
For the hour of their births, a cross
For the hour of their deaths. Grave after
Grave, row after crooked row like fields
Of rotting corn.
              My eyes fall
On words: *Para mi querido hijo*, a mother's
Final letter to her war-dead son. The foreigner
Has found a place, died for a flag that knows only
How to wave *adios* in English. A broken angel,
Wingless, protects the grave of an infant
Whose name the wind has stolen.
                      A cloud
Covers the sun. It will not rain. I stand
In this noonday darkness somewhere between
A cross and a star, strip off my clothes, rags
That hide my bones. Bones. Bones fighting to bare
Their blankness to open air. I strip, listen
To the sound of my skin scrape against the earth,
And dance to the music of the only instrument
I ever learned to play: the dirt. The silent,
Too silent, biographer, the earth. The earth.

Sacrifices

Mesilla Park, New Mexico
May, 1962

We are in the center, my brother and I. Our hair
Cut so short, it stands straight. Shiny, it glitters,
Catches light. *If only they had let us*
Grow our hair long.

On this late spring Sunday, we pose
Holding candles, black prayer books, plastic rosaries. Ribbons
Tied to right arms, white and swaying like large leaves
Wanting to tear free of the tree. *If only there was life*
Without the tree. Our white shirts, new, respectfully worn;
Our black pants pressed with perfect lines from Mama's iron.
Our clothes stiff; we yearn to strip. Today,
We must endure them.

Our smiles restrained. Having eaten
Of the bread, partaken of the sacrifice we witnessed on the altar,
Adults now. We saw. We took. We ate. Adults, having tasted
The Catholic God. Our tongues still tingling from the touch
Of the white host. Today we are good. Today, we take our place, follow
The path that has been worn down by the generations before us
To make our travels lighter. *If only we could walk*
Another road. Today, we step.
Safe.

Pushing and pulling, our grandmothers behind us:
Tall statues with thinning hair. Skin already eroded
By their many rituals of sacrifice. Statues no longer worshipped
By men, but perfect for boyhood love. Their hands
On our shoulders pushing us down towards earth, pulling us
Up towards sky. We, newly harvested corn,
Perfect offerings for their hungry God.

A Killing

Las Cruces, New Mexico
February 10, 1990

LAS CRUCES—Nearly 1,000 mourners filled Immaculate Heart of Mary Cathedral Tuesday for the funeral of Amy Houser, one of four Las Crucens slain in a robbery. Saturday morning, two gunmen entered the bowling alley, rounded up Houser and six others, and shot each twice in the back of the head as they lay on the floor.

for Gloria

What she made in her body is broken.

Lost, she searches, everywhere, for news
of her daughter. She looks with want,
her hunger controls her now. *Is she hurt—*
my Amy? I want to reach my fist down my throat
and force out the word that is
food: *She is alive.* I want to hand her
this banquet, serve her, watch her feast
on the goodness.

         I ache for sleep
but she disturbs. She comes to me.
She is running out of the bakery still
wearing her apron, stained
from her morning work. She who bakes
today will not see the bread rise.
She is in tears, but the salt
that flows from within her
seasons her face with hope.

She waits for news, arms ready
to hold again. She reaches,
breaks through a barricade in front
of that place—a shooting. She grabs
a policeman's arm making him show
his face—I see that it is me. *Is she hurt?*

                  I feel her
body against mine as she digs her whole
self into me—a root clinging to soil
but the soil is spent. Her howl
is a wind that runs through me
daily—blows my blood like sand
and I become a desert that knows only
thirst. I see her taking my face between
her hands—her smile holding the question.
Patient, she waits for an answer. *Come,
woman, I will take you to her tomb. You
will see that it is empty.* We go to the place
where they have laid her. But I am not
strong enough to roll back the stone.

Waking to Winter

Las Cruces, New Mexico
Lent, 1990

Every day they cry. For her. Their girl,
First grandchild, first-born fruit of the orchard
they planted in youth. Girl who gave them names,
Who made words new again. Girl who was spring in their
Autumn, who taught them to laugh, to love again. This is what
They longed for: to wake and see their fields
Ablaze in blooms, watered in the sweat of their labor.

∙

Since I was born, my father has cried twice:
Once for his mother. And now, for the child who would never
Leave children grieving at her grave. *How could they kill her?*
My mother watches him, her arms reaching to hold him,
Her heart holding fast to the picture of her girl
Who is present in their room now only as memory.

∙

He is afraid for his wife, is afraid now
When she goes out at night. He dreams of the gun aimed
Straight at this granddaughter's head. He feels the bullet
Enter as if it were entering *him*. He wakes and watches
His wife. *She is asleep. She is safe.* Next day,
On her way to the store, she stops to see a friend.
She is gone from the house for hours. In a moment
Of madness, he begs my brother to go and search

For her. Panic holds him now. *They have taken her. They*
Have taken her, too. When she arrives back home, he yells at her
Then cries. *Don't go out alone, not at night, not alone.*

·

Tired, my mother falls asleep. She is dreaming of the day
The little girl was born. She sees herself handing
The blood of her blood, the flesh of her flesh
To her husband. Not even his mustache, dark and thick
As the night, can hide his joy. Today, they wake
To winter. Just yesterday, everywhere sun, no wind
In sight. The spring was false. The buds, just born,
Are dead. No fruit this year. The land is bare. The cold
Has stripped the fields.

Easter

Mesilla, New Mexico
Spring, 1962

My mother woke us that Sunday—her voice
a bell proclaiming spring. We rose
diving into our clothes, newly bought.
We took turns standing before mirrors,
combing, staring at our new selves.
Sinless from forty days of desert,
sinless from good confessions, we
drove to church in a red pickup, bright
and red and waxed for the special
occasion. Clean, polished as apples,
the yellow-dressed girls in front
with Mom and Dad; the boys in back,
our hair blowing free in the warming
wind. Winter gone away. At Mass,
the choir singing loud: ragged
notes from ragged angels' voices;
ancient hymns sung in crooked Latin.
The priest, white-robed, raised his palms
toward God, opened his mouth in awe:
"Alleluia!" The unspoken word of Lent
let loose in flight. Alleluia and incense
rising, my mother wiping her tears
from words she'd heard; my brother and I
whispering names of statues lining
the walls of the church. Bells ringing,

Mass ending, we running to the truck,
shiny as shoes going dancing. Dad
driving us to see my grandmother. There,
at her house, I asked about the new word
I'd heard: *resurrection*. "Death,
death," she said, her hands moving downward,
"the cross—*that* is death." And then she
laughed: "The dead will rise." Her upturned
palms moved skyward as she spoke. "The dead
will rise." She moved her hands toward me,
wrapped my face with touches, and
laughed again. *The dead will rise.*

The Return

New Mexico
1864–1868

Like all Indians the Navajos prefer their own country
and it is quite natural they should. Yet in view of the
past experience of the Government with, and the well
known history of, this tribe, they should never again
be permitted to return to their former homes.

SPECIAL AGENT GRAVES

1864–1867

Once lords of earth,
now kept like sheep.
More than three years
they remained at *Hwelte*,
for *Fuerte*, "Strong place"
with strong fences.

Bureaucracies argued.
What should be done
with the conquered?
After the war was won,
New Man was lost
in politics.
Solutions, far away
as rain. Debates
flew like bullets
landing in New Man's newspapers.

The Navajo waited,
ate food condemned
by soldiers as unfit,
food New Man would not
pass through his lips.
A new system was devised
(for every problem,
a government resolution):
One pound of food
for each man, woman, and child
per day. One pound
of corn, or flour, or beans.
On this, the people
filled themselves, gathered strength
to dig, to plant
rows of corn and wheat.
On this, they labored.

In late summer of 1864,
the crops failed.
In 1865, the crops failed.
Some escaped. Those who fled
by night, died, but died
flying towards Dinetah.
Some reached the land
of the living: Dinetah.
In 1867, the crops failed.
The Navajo cried:
"This land is Godless,
never ours. We cannot
live here—Godless.

We labor in vain.
We cannot live
where the ground
is sterile and cursed!
We want our lands
if only to bury our dead."

1868

It was agreed:
the people were to return
to Dinetah, the place
where souls could breathe,
where crops could grow.
The treaty was prepared.
Monday, the first day
in June
two commissioners of peace
and the leaders of the people
gathered to sign:
clear signatures spelling out
the names of the literate,
and X's for all the rest.

At dawn
that June
the Navajo journeyed
to their lands.
Their line stretched
for miles,
stretching towards Dinetah.

The gravity of home
pulling their scarred
souls towards an earth
whose arms reached
across deserts.
Their eyes not seeing
weeds or sand
but Dinetah.
They walked in stillness,
walked in prayer,
walked in light
and silence:

*There is something within us which does not speak but thinks,
and though we remain silent, our faces speak to one another.*

*Cage the badger and he will try to break from his prison and
regain his native hold. Chain the eagle to the ground—he will
strive to regain his freedom, and though he fails, he will lift
his head and look up to the sky which is his home. And we want
to return to our mountains and our meadows.*

Prodigal Men

―――

Las Cruces, New Mexico
December, 1989

Who were dead, are alive again.

He has come back, who was gone,
Has come home to find rest. Nearing ninety, his sight
No longer clear, his hearing almost gone, the old man
Who is father to my father has returned.

∎

Work came easy to him, but love did not.
He taught me to worship a hoe, respect the tools of men.
He sliced the grounds of his garden at angles, perfect,
The weeds fell helpless before his easy strokes.
To him, this flawless labor was a prayer. "Hands
and legs, arms and back must move as one. Watch close—like this."
Then handed me the hoe. I imagined the weeds were trees:
Chop, chop, thud. Chop, chop, thud. Tim-berrr! "No
Daydreaming! Keep your mind on your work. Work
Is the secret to life, the secret to being a man."
But six-year-old eyes were in love with the fruits
Not the labor, the grapes, not the picking. "I want
To play," I told him. "Play, play, ha!" he said, "Work."

∎

His wife fed us food and forgiveness. She knew
About boys, about men, and knew the needs of both.
When she grew weak, I begged her to live. "Take him
Instead!" I'd pray, preferred his death to hers—
And cursed God for his choice. She left us poor,
Left us before we had learned the necessary skill of love.

∎

No longer husband to anyone I loved, he met a woman,
Took her dancing, disappeared in a life of second
Chances. As if to divorce the past (or perhaps
Divorce his grief), he stopped arriving for dinner,
Decided he was done with former duties.

                           At Christmas, I always sent
A gift. *Once a year? A gift? Only a gift?* I nodded
At my father. "I'll try and go to see him."

                                   ■

       *"For twenty years I lived with
Her family. When she got sick, I was in the way.
Treated like a dog, I said, 'Treat me with respect,'
But they ignored my words. I told them I was leaving,
That I was going back."*

                                   ■

                           I, too, returned
To that house where we first met. Twenty-one years
Since I'd set foot on his soil. Through the window
In the door, I could see him sitting on a chair,
His jacket on. I didn't knock, turned the knob
Unlocked. He looked up, confused and lost, but when
I spoke, he smiled. Shouting my childhood name
He embraced me hard, then fell back tired on the chair.

    We sat together, spoke quick, no silence now
Between us. "She laughed often as a girl, my Josefina.
I had to beg—for months—for her to marry me. And when
She died, went crazy, left my job too soon."

                            He talked of life
In Texas, of his youth and days of work. "Don't grow much
Cotton anymore, was hard to pick." He pounded on a wall:
"They're strong," he said, "I built this house to last,
Made it of adobe, of the earth." He led me through his house
As if I'd never seen it. Few furnishings, her
Statues gone.

                    Outside, we walked abandoned grounds, once
His summer garden. Where once there were perfect rows,
He kicked the earth. I watch his loosening skin, worn
Thin by years and losses. More lines on his old face
Than strokes in van Gogh's paintings. For a moment, we stopped
Exchanging memories. He looked at me, and I looked back—our eyes
Stared long. "You look like her," he said, "like Josefina."

Resurrections

California
Lent, 1990

The stones themselves will sing.

Broken, Incan roads. The stones laid perfect
on mountains of snow so stubborn
not even blazing suns could beat it into water.
But the Incans could tame such mountains. With a fire
of their own, they knew how to melt that ice.
Stone by stone, step by step, the ancients
walked the highest paths of earth. Stones,
tight knots that tied the world together. Roads, higher—
now stones are buried deep like bones
of Incan lords. I walked there barefoot
on cold stones. Those roads were perfect once again
until I woke. Those roads, like Incan hands
who built them, refuse to lie still
in the ground. They loosen the wasted land.

∙

My mother lost him young, her older brother. She gave
my brother his name "because the moment he was born
his name rose to my lips." Ricardo, "A friend
took a stone, and broke his skull wide open—
and broke my mother's heart." She walks with him
on a path they took to school. There, in the sun, he laughs
until she wakes. Been forty years,
and grief is glued to her. Anger rises
in her voice: "But *here*," she grabs his picture,
"*Here* he is perfect. *Here* he is not broken."

∙

The beer I drink is good tonight,
almost sweet, but cold. The dead are close.
Calm, I sit, touch the photographs of those
I walked with. Grandparents, uncles, not one
generation was spared. A brother. A niece.
In the country of their final exile
their legs will not cross the border.
Their feet will not touch my earth again
but tonight I hear their steps. I swallow,
must finish the beer I have started. *Take this*
all of you and drink. This is my blood. Tired,
I drink from the cup, take the cold, within me now,
and wrap myself in faces of the dead:
stones which form a path where I walk still.

.

The Mimbres buried their dead beneath their homes.
At night, softly, the buried
rose, re-entered the rooms of the living
as blankets woven with the heavy threads of memory,
blankets on which the Mimbres rested,
on which they slept, and dreamed.

Notes on the Poems

Creation ▪ I owe the writing of this poem to Richard Rhodes. His book *The Making of the Atomic Bomb* (Simon and Schuster, 1986) inspired it.

Exiled ▪ The italicized portion of the poem is an actual newspaper account taken from *A Journey Through Texas*. The citation was quoted, along with descriptions of exiled *Tejanos*, in David Montejano's *Anglos and Mexicans in the Making of Texas, 1836–1986* (University of Texas Press, 1987).

Walking ▪ The italicized portions of the poem are taken from "Navajo Night Chants," a traditional Navajo poem.

Parades ▪ The song "O Johnny Navajo" was actually sung by the "army" gathered by Kit Carson to fight the Navajo as it marched out of Taos. Taken from *Lords of the Earth* by Jules Loh (Crowell-Collier, 1971).

Poem ▪ The epigraph is by Emily Dickinson. From poem 441 in *The Complete Poems of Emily Dickinson*, edited by Thomas H. Johnson (Little, Brown, 1960).

A New Flag ▪ The italicized passages ascribed to General Kearny are taken from a speech he made as he took possession of New Mexico.

Workers ▪ The poem is based on an actual account of a Mexican farm-worker. I read the account in Montejano's *Anglos and Mexicans in the Making of Texas*.

A Killing ▪ *What she made in her body is broken* is the first line of a poem entitled "For J." by Wendell Berry. From *The Country of Marriage* (Harcourt Brace Jovanovich, 1973).

The Return ▪ The final stanza is the "voice" of an anonymous Navajo. The account was recorded in government documents.

About the Author

Benjamin Alire Sáenz grew up in the desert of southern New Mexico, deeply aware of the landscape and of his Chicano heritage. He earned a master's degree from the University of Louvain in Belgium in theology, and a master's degree in creative writing from the University of Texas at El Paso. In 1988 he was awarded a Wallace E. Stegner fellowship in poetry at Stanford University. He currently lives in Menlo Park, California.

Design by Ken Sánchez.

Text set in Electra by G&S Typesetters, Inc., Austin, Texas.

Printed on acid-free paper and Smyth sewn
by Malloy Lithographing, Inc., Ann Arbor, Michigan.